# Goldilocks and the Three Bears

Retold and dramatised as a reading play
for partners or small groups.

Ellie Hallett

# Ways to read this story

This story is suitable for school and home. Some 'how to read' ideas are below.

- With a partner or small group, take it in turns to read the rows.

- Don't rush! This helps you to say each word clearly.

- Think of yourselves as actors by adding lots of facial and vocal expression. Small gaps of silence also create dramatic energy. These techniques will bring the story to life.

- If you meet a new word, try to break it down and then say it again. If you have any problems, ask your teacher or a reading buddy.

- Don't be scared of unusual words. They will become your new best friends.
(New words strengthen your general knowledge and enable you to become vocabulary-rich in your day-to-day life.)

Have fun!

Once upon a time there was a little girl whose name was Goldilocks.

In case you are wondering, the word *locks* is another name for hair.

Goldilocks loved going for walks in the early morning before the sun became too hot.

One Saturday morning, while the dew was still on the grass, she decided to explore a new path through the woods.

It wasn't very long before she came across a charming country cottage.

**'Mmmm! I can smell something, and I think it's my favourite breakfast - oatmeal porridge.'**

**'I'll knock on the door and ask politely if I can have a taste.'**

But when Goldilocks knocked on the front door, there was no answer.

She waited and listened, but all was quiet.

With the thought of delicious porridge on her mind, she gave the door a little push.

To her surprise, it opened as if it was meant to open.

'I shouldn't go inside a house while the owners are away, but I'm very hungry!'

'If I can find where the porridge is, I'll just have a little taste and then go home.'

As we all know, this cottage belonged to a family called The Three Bears.

The bears were out having their usual morning walk in the fresh air while their breakfast was cooling.

Each of the bears loved these walks for different reasons.

Baby Bear worked on his tree-climbing skills. He knew the sweetest berries always grew on the highest branches.

Mother Bear constantly sniffed the air. She was searching for the scent of wild honey.

Father Bear walked and then stopped, walked and then stopped.

While he was stopped, he listened.

He wanted to hear if salmon were jumping over the rapids in the nearby river.

Meanwhile, back in The Three Bears' cottage, Goldilocks was very busy.

'First I'll try the porridge in the big bowl.
Ouch! Oh no – far too hot.'

'Now I'll try the porridge in the middle-
sized bowl. Ugh! Oh no – far too cold.'

'Ah yes! The porridge in the smallest bowl
looks just right. I'll have just one little
spoonful before I go straight home ...'

**'… and now perhaps just one more.'**

And before long, naughty Goldilocks had eaten the whole lot.

Feeling much better after such a delicious breakfast, Goldilocks decided to look around the cottage.

It was beautifully cosy and warm.

Morning sunshine streamed in through the windows, making everything sparkle.

Into the sitting room went Goldilocks, where she saw three fine-looking chairs.

**'I think I'll try them out quickly for size and comfort.'**

**'First I'll sit in this large high-backed chair. Oh no! Far too hard.'**

**'Perhaps this middle-sized armchair is better. Oh no no no! Far too soft.'**

**'Ah yes! This dear little baby chair looks just right.'**

**'Oops! Oh no! Hmmm ... I've broken it.'**

**'Perhaps it *was* a bit too small for me after all.'**

And she left the chair lying on the floor with its legs quite broken while she kept on walking around the cottage.

**'While I'm here, I may as well have a look upstairs. It won't take a moment, and then I'll go straight home.'**

So upstairs she went.

**'Oh, what beautiful beds, and each one as neat as a bed is possible to be.'**

**'I'll just try out each one quickly, and then I'll go home.'**

**'First I'll try this super-sized king bed. Oh no. Far too high!'**

**'Next I'll try this queen-sized bed. Oh no no no. Far too low!'**

**'Ah, yes! This little bed looks just right - and - it is!'**

'I'll close my eyes for just one minute, and then I'll run as fast as I can back down the path until I reach home.'

Meanwhile, outside in the sunshine, The Three Bears had almost arrived home after their long morning walk.

Each bear was making plans for the day.

Father Bear spoke first in his slow, deep, rumbling voice.

'After I eat my porridge, I'm going to read my new book all about salmon.'

Mother Bear was the next to speak in her smooth, silky voice.

'After breakfast I'm going to make a honey cake with all the trimmings.'

Baby Bear had his say in a high and excited sort of voice.

'I'm totally starving! I am going to eat all my porridge and then sit in my little chair and draw some wild raspberries.'

But as soon as the bears walked up to their front door, they stopped and looked at each other.

Each bear felt there was something wrong.

'I think we have had a visitor!'

'Now that's very strange! Our front door is wide open.'

'I hope whoever it is hasn't touched any of my things or looked at my berry drawing books.'

And into the cottage they went, walking and looking and thinking deeply at the same time.

Father Bear saw at once that their cottage looked rather messy.

**'Someone's been eating from my bowl of porridge and they've spilt little bits of it all over the tablecloth.'**

Mother Bear gasped in surprise when she saw her bowl of porridge.

**'Someone's been eating my porridge and they've left sticky finger marks all over the bowl and spoon.'**

Baby Bear stared in amazement at his bowl of porridge. He cried out in a very loud voice ...

**'Waa-aa-aa! Someone's eaten my porridge all up and there isn't even one mouthful left for me. Waa-aa!'**

Father Bear checked Baby Bear's bowl.

Sure enough, all that remained on the bottom of the bowl were scrape marks and a used porridge spoon.

By now The Three Bears were very worried.

They decided to check the drawing room.
Father Bear spoke first.

**'Someone's been sitting in my chair, and my new book on salmon has been tossed onto the floor.'**

Mother Bear spoke next.

**'Someone's been sitting in my chair and crumpled my lovely soft cushions.'**

Baby Bear started crying again as he stared in disbelief at what he saw.

**'Someone's been sitting in my chair, and, and, and they've broken it to bits. Waa-aa.'**

Mother and Father Bear hurried over to look at Baby Bear's chair. It was definitely broken.

The Three Bears were now more worried than ever.

They decided to go upstairs to see if there was any more damage.

Halfway up the stairs, Father Bear whispered to himself in a raspy voice.

**'I hope whoever it is hasn't taken my favourite pocket watch.'**

Mother Bear spoke to herself in a quietly frightened sort of voice.

**'I hope it isn't a burglar waiting for us with a big stick to hit us on the head.'**

Baby Bear heard his mother and replied in a baby sort of brave voice …

**'If they have a big stick, I'll tell them to put it down at once and go home.'**

And so slowly up the stairs they crept, none of them knowing what they might find.

They could scarcely believe their eyes when they walked into the bedroom.

Father Bear spoke first in a very cross voice.

**'Someone's been sleeping in my bed and left the covers all over the floor.'**

Mother Bear spoke next in a very annoyed sort of voice.

**'Someone's been sleeping in my bed and muddled up all my soft pillows.'**

Baby Bear then called out in a voice louder than he had ever used before.

**'Someone's been sleeping in my bed and put a great big lump in it.'**

Suddenly the great big lump sat up and spoke.

**'Oh my goodness! Where am I? Why am I in a strange bed?'**

Father Bear growled a very long growl. With a big frown on his face, he spoke in his most serious Father Bear voice.

**'Why are you in our house, little girl, and why are you in Baby Bear's bed?**

Mother Bear bent forward and asked a question in a gentle Mother Bear voice.

**'Didn't your parents teach you not to go into houses that weren't yours?'**

But before Goldilocks could answer, Baby Bear had the longest question of all.

He spoke in a voice that stopped and started because he was trying not to cry.

**'And didn't you know that it is bad manners to eat someone else's - waa-aa - breakfast, and then sit in their chair and break it, and, and - waa-aa - climb into their bed and go to sleep?'**

It was now Goldilocks' turn to speak. By now she was fully awake.

'I'm really sorry, Three Bears. My name is Goldilocks. I smelt your porridge and just had to come in.'

'I know now that I shouldn't have touched your porridge, sat in your chairs or tried out your beds.'

'And Baby Bear, I am truly sorry that I ate your breakfast, broke your little chair and then fell asleep in your bed.'

'My parents taught me that if I am the cause of a problem, I must fix it.'

'And so I promise to pay you for all the damage I have done.'

When she arrived home, she told her parents everything that had happened.

They agreed with her plan to make amends for what she had done.

And so every day for two months, Goldilocks did all the jobs she could find.

She cleaned out the bird cage and washed the dog's food bowl.

She scrubbed the kitchen floor until it shone like sunshine.

She polished the silver and set the table for every meal.

She watered the garden and planted strawberries for Baby Bear.

Most surprising of all, she kept her room as tidy as two new pins.

After two months, she returned to The Three Bears' cottage with the presents she had bought with the money she had earned.

To Father Bear she gave a book called *How to Catch Salmon Quickly.*

To Mother Bear she gave a large jar of *Busy Bee Honey* and a big glossy recipe book called *Best Ever Honey Cakes.*

And for Baby Bear, she had not one, not two, but three presents.

The first one was a basket of fresh strawberries and a jar of cream.

The second one was a cuddly teddy bear that looked exactly like Baby Bear.

And the third one was a new chair exactly like the one she had broken.

Best of all, though, Goldilocks introduced her parents to The Three Bears, and they became good friends.

You will be also pleased to know that Goldilocks didn't ever go into someone else's house without being invited!

Using these pictures, retell the story in your own words.

Change your voice to sound like the character who is speaking.